THE BOOK OF JOB

Rose Visual Bible Studies

ROSE
PUBLISHING

Rose Visual Bible Studies
The Book of Job

Copyright © 2024 by Rose Publishing
Published by Rose Publishing
An imprint of Tyndale House Ministries
Carol Stream, Illinois
hendricksonrose.com

ISBN 978-1-4964-9036-0

Author: Titus O'Bryant, ThM, Senior Pastor, LifePoint Church, Reisterstown, MD

Excerpt from *The Velveteen Rabbit* adapted from Margery Williams, *The Velveteen Rabbit: Or How Toys Become Real* (London: Heinemann, 1922) (public domain).

Printed in the United States of America
010324VP

Contents

There once was a man named Job
who lived in the land of Uz.
He was blameless—
a man of complete integrity.
He feared God and stayed away from evil.

Job 1:1

The Book of Job

Mystery. Who doesn't like a good tale filled with suspense? Authors of mystery novels demonstrate a unique skill to weave excellent stories. By dropping details and withholding key information until just the right moment, they are able to captivate readers, inspire filmmakers, and sell lots of whodunit books. Perhaps they learned from the book of Job.

Job was a man whose life flourished with security and significance: He was a man of excellent character who enjoyed a good reputation and exerted influence on others. His children had reached adulthood and were thriving. He was prosperous and looked forward to a comfortable future. But in a moment, he lost it all—his wealth, his family, his health. Even his reputation came under assault. Job was left with a heart full of pain and a head full of questions: *Who is responsible? How could this happen to me? Why would God allow this?*

Have you ever asked questions like these? Mysteries can be entertaining to read but confusing and painful to live. Although we can have a relationship with God through his Son, Jesus Christ, there is still so much about God that remains a mystery to us. However long we journey through life, some of our experiences never quite make sense. That is why God gave us the book of Job. While Job's story may not answer every question we have, studying his story can help us hold on to faith and hope while living through life's mysteries.

Over the six sessions of this study, we will journey with Job to discover how he endured his unexpected hardships and still emerged with his faith and integrity intact. We'll see how Job was honest about his pain, questioned his beliefs, argued with others about his suffering, and ultimately bowed in worship to our sovereign God. The book of Job can help us understand and navigate our own experiences of pain and suffering.

1

JOB'S PAIN

*The Power of
Crying Out*

Job's Pain

Does the expression "crying out" inspire a particular image in your mind—perhaps an infant expressing discomfort or fear, a child throwing a tantrum, a teenager lamenting their first breakup, or an adult breaking down under a crushing load of stress? Job was a righteous man who suffered deep loss and pain through no fault of his own.

The book of Job explores suffering through (1) realities that remain hidden from Job's perspective, (2) the reasonings of Job's friends, (3) Job's vulnerability and honest complaints, and (4) a glimpse of God's perspective on our human condition. His experience reminds us that some of the finest people seem to endure the most misery. Yet "in all of this, Job did not sin by blaming God" (Job 1:22). Instead, Job cried out to God while he was weeping.

Read It

Key Bible Passage

Read Job 1:1–2:13, detailing surprising scenes in heaven and Job's testings, losses, and responses.

Optional Reading

Read Psalm 142, a song of David crying out to the Lord for rescue.

If you would like to read through the entire book of Job over the course of this six-session Bible study, you can follow the daily reading plan provided for each of the six sessions.

Book of Job Reading Plan

- ❏ **Day 1:** Job chapter 1
- ❏ **Day 2:** Job chapter 2
- ❏ **Day 3:** Job chapter 3
- ❏ **Day 4:** Job chapter 4
- ❏ **Day 5:** Job chapter 5
- ❏ **Day 6:** Job chapter 6
- ❏ **Day 7:** Job chapter 7

Job stood up and tore his robe in grief. Then he shaved his head and fell to the ground to worship.

JOB 1:20

Know It

1. In Job 1:9–11, what conclusions does Satan make about the reasons people trust and worship God?

2. In Job 1:20–22, what do you observe about Job's response to his initial loss? How does this prove or disprove Satan's conclusions?

3. After reading this first scene in the book of Job, what questions do you have and what do you want to know more about?

Job: Parable or History?

Did the events of Job actually happen, or is the book of Job an elaborate parable designed to teach timeless truth? Bible scholars have taken various positions on viewing Job as a wisdom parable or a true-life story.

Some of the factors for considering Job a **parable** include:

- The opening scene is a heavenly one where Satan and the Lord seem engaged in polite conversation.

- The series of dialogues between Job and his friends are highly stylized and poetic.

- In the closing scene, Job receives twice what he had lost, and he had seven more sons and three daughters.

Some reasons to consider the story of Job as **history** include:

- The prophet Ezekiel and James, leader of the early Jerusalem church, seem to consider Job to be historical (Ezekiel 14:14, 20; James 5:11).

- Parables in the Bible do not normally include names of the characters.

- There is no clear indication in the book that the narrative is anything other than historical fact.

Whichever way you view Job, the truth of the book remains the same: Job reminds us there are limits to our understanding, and it teaches us how to maintain our faith during troubling times. Most importantly, it helps us appreciate the sovereignty of our God over every part of life.

Time Period for the Book of Job

As with many other aspects of the book of Job that are difficult to decipher, the date of writing and the identity of the author are uncertain.

Early Date: 15th century BC or earlier

The story of Job might be set around the time of the Israelite patriarchs Abraham, Isaac, and Jacob because:

- The book includes no mention of the Mosaic law or the Israelites.

- Job offers his own sacrifices rather than participating in the Levitical sacrificial system.

- Job's lifespan (more than 140 years according to Job 42:16) is similar to others recorded in the Bible during this time period.

- Job's wealth was measured by livestock rather than land or other means, similar to the custom during the time of Abraham and the other patriarchs.

Job's story could have been an oral tradition passed down through generations and then recorded by Moses or an unnamed writer.

Late Date: 6th through 4th centuries BC

Some features of the book fit better with a later date, around the time of the Jewish exile in the Persian Empire, because:

- The Hebrew used in Job has signs of influence from Aramaic, the common language during the Persian era.

- The word *satan* is used with the Hebrew definite article (Job 1:6; 2:1), which doesn't happen again until Zechariah's prophecies in the sixth century BC.

- The Jewish people suffered greatly during this era, as evidenced by contemporary prophetic books such as Isaiah and Jeremiah. The theme of suffering in Job could speak directly to the suffering of God's people during the times of Isaiah and Jeremiah.

It's even possible that arguments for both an early *and* a late date have some validity: Job could have been recorded at an early date by Moses or a different author, but a later editor could have made adjustments that reflect a later time period.

The Land of Uz (not Oz)

Job was introduced as a man "who lived in the land of Uz" (Job 1:1). The prophet Jeremiah gives us the best clues for spotting this land and identifying Job's heritage. In Jeremiah 25:19–25, Jeremiah prophesies of coming judgment against all the kingdoms of the world, including his own nation, Judah, and its surrounding nations: Egypt, Philistia, Phoenicia, Arabia, Babylon, Edom, and Uz. In the book of Lamentations, most likely written by Jeremiah, he writes about Edom's reaction to God's judgment against Judah, asking, "Are you rejoicing in the land of Uz, O people of Edom?" (4:21). Thus, traditionally Uz has been closely associated with the Edomites, who were descendants of Jacob's twin brother, Esau.

Aravah Valley, Israel, near the ancient land of Edom

The most likely geographic location for Uz is somewhere southeast of the Dead Sea. This region is close to but separate

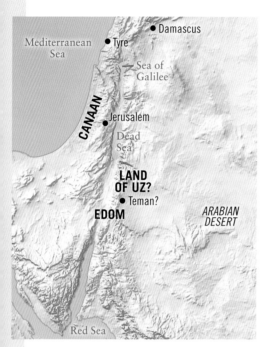

from the land God promised to Jacob's descendants in Canaan. The mention of the Sabean and Chaldean raiding bands that stole Job's livestock suggests a non-Jewish setting located in northern Arabia or southwestern Jordan (Job 1:15, 17). The Chaldeans came from ancient Babylon (modern Iraq) and spread across the Middle East, while the Sabeans were a nomadic tribe from southern Arabia. Job's flocks and herds would have been within striking distance of both of these nomadic groups.

The Heavenly Court

Job chapters 1 and 2 present a unique scene in heaven, where "members of the heavenly court" are gathered, including "the Accuser, Satan" (Job 1:6; 2:1). What is meant by the term *heavenly court*, and who was part of this court? Equally intriguing is the question, Why would Satan—an angelic being who rebelled against God—be present at this heavenly court?

To answer these questions, let's start by looking at the culture that surrounded the Israelites. (Though the setting for Job is likely just outside of ancient Israel, the viewpoint is thoroughly Israelite as part of the Hebrew Scriptures.) Spreading from the Mediterranean Sea through the Jordan River valley were the Canaanite people groups. They were known for worshiping the false god named Baal, as well as other gods who sat at different levels in a "heavenly" court. At the top was El and his wife; next was El's chief steward, Baal, who carried out El's wishes; and below Baal were many other gods responsible for parts of nature or commerce or served as messengers between gods.

The Israelites were influenced by this surrounding culture for centuries and often tried to include Baal worship alongside their worship of the one true God, Yahweh. Some commentators argue that the heavenly court in Job is an example of this dynamic, reflecting how the Israelites shared a common worldview that included a court for godlike beings.

CANAANITE "HEAVENLY COURT" STRUCTURE

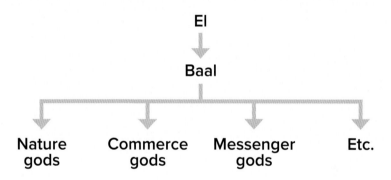

However, there is a better explanation that aligns strongly with God's command in the Scriptures that "you must not have any other god but me" (Exodus 20:3). In Job 1:6 and 2:1, the phrase "members of the heavenly court" (NLT) or "the angels" (NIV) or "the sons of God" (ESV) is translated from a Hebrew phrase that includes the word *Elohim*. Words in the biblical Hebrew language often have a wide range of meanings. Over two thousand times in the Old Testament, *Elohim* refers to the God of Israel, whose personal name is Yahweh. Less frequently, *Elohim* refers to a pagan god or spiritual being. For example:

- Demons who received sacrifices from idolatrous Israelites (Deuteronomy 32:17)

- A being ascending from the underworld, which frightened the witch of Endor (1 Samuel 28:13)

- The gods of foreign nations (1 Kings 11:33)

- Heavenly beings who appear in heaven's court, where God presides (Psalm 82:1)

The Scriptures are clear that there is only one God, so the heavenly court seems to be made up of heavenly beings, normally called angels, who were created by God to be his servants and messengers. It's even possible to imagine how Satan, as a fallen angel, could have been included in this kind of gathering.

Based on Job's mention of a heavenly court or the usage of the word *Elohim*, there is no reason to assume the scenarios in Job 1:6 and 2:1 are similar to Canaanite Baal worship. And even though there is a spiritual world that is currently hidden from our perception, we have no need to fear this world or become distracted with unnecessary speculation about the unseen realm.

Satan

The Hebrew word *satan* generally means accuser, opposer, or adversary. Job 1:6 is the first place in the Bible where in Hebrew it is used as a name or title. As a created angelic being who rebelled against God, Satan's purpose is to oppose God and destroy everything he made.

Although he is not always named, Satan is connected to a few other Old Testament chapters, including Genesis 3, where the serpent in the garden of Eden tempts Eve to disobey God. Isaiah 14 and Ezekiel 28 tell stories about God's judgment coming to earthly kings (Babylon and Tyre, respectively), but some believe these passages may also reference Satan's fall from heaven after he rebelled and God cast him out.

Notice the similarity in language between the following Old Testament passages and the New Testament passages that connect them to the identity of Satan:

OLD TESTAMENT	NEW TESTAMENT
"The **serpent** was the **shrewdest** of all the wild animals the LORD God had made. One day he asked the woman, 'Did God really say you must not eat the fruit from any of the trees in the garden?'" (Genesis 3:1)	"This great dragon—the **ancient serpent** called the devil, or Satan, the one deceiving the whole world—was **thrown down to the earth** with all his angels." (Revelation 12:9)
"How you are **fallen from heaven**, O shining star, son of the morning! You have been **thrown down to the earth**, you who destroyed the nations of the world." (Isaiah 14:12)	"When the seventy-two disciples returned, they joyfully reported to [Jesus], 'Lord, even the demons obey us when we use your name!' 'Yes,' he told them, 'I saw **Satan fall from heaven** like lightning!'" (Luke 10:17–18)
"I ordained and anointed you as the mighty angelic guardian. You had access to the holy mountain of God and walked among the stones of fire. You were blameless in all you did from the day you were created until the day **evil was found in you**." (Ezekiel 28:14–15)	"[The devil] was a murderer from the beginning. He has always hated the truth, because there is no truth in him. **When he lies, it is consistent with his character**; for he is a liar and the father of lies." (John 8:44)

Satan rules over fallen angels, exerts power over the systems of this world, tempts people to sin, and works to destroy lives—all because he hates God and his people. Just as Job encountered this enemy, we today are also subject to his evil influence.

Cry Out

Following his devastating losses, Job cried out to God, fully expressing his pain and disappointment, his mistrust and wounded faith, his confident integrity, and his questioning trust. After seven days of silence, Job used powerfully descriptive words to describe how he felt: "I cannot eat for sighing; my groans pour out like water" (Job 3:24).

"Sighing" is translated from the Hebrew word *anakhah*, and "groans" is translated from the Hebrew word *sheh'agah*, which describes a powerfully loud crying out, likened to the roaring of a lion or bellowing in rage or pain. Both Hebrew words are used by David in the Psalms when he writes about crying out with sighs, sobs, and groans amid his suffering (Psalm 6:6; 31:10; 32:3). In Psalm 22:1, David wrote, "My God, my God, why have you abandoned me? Why are you so far away when I **groan** [*sheh'agah*] for help?" Jesus spoke the first part of this verse as he experienced the sighing and groaning that accompanied his painful death (Matthew 27:46; Mark 15:34).

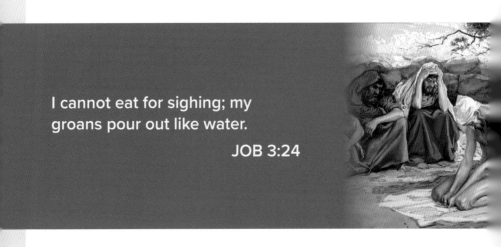

I cannot eat for sighing; my groans pour out like water.

JOB 3:24

It's interesting to note that life begins with a cry. Inside the womb, a baby's lungs are collapsed and airless while needed oxygen is delivered through the mother's blood. But as an infant is delivered, the pressure around their rib cage drops dramatically. This causes the expansion and unfolding of respiratory system tissues that were previously collapsed. For most infants, this means a forceful inhalation followed by exhalation against their partially closed voice box—somewhat like blowing through a partially closed pipe. Small air sacs then pop open as air is forcefully moved into the lungs. The result? A cry! Considering the baby is also in a new environment with bright lights, new sounds, and different temperatures, it's only natural to cry.

Although life begins with a cry, we are trained *not* to cry out as we grow older. We learn to avoid or deny pain that catches us by surprise. We discover how to hide our weakness by pretending we don't really hurt. But just as crying out brings inner life to infants as they breathe in oxygen and expel carbon dioxide, the ability to cry out to God effectively when life wounds us can help expel the toxins that build up in our souls and receive in return the breath of God into our lives. Crying out to God with brutal honesty expresses a deep and abiding faith (however weak or tested that faith may be). It shows we trust that God is listening and will respond by demonstrating his faithfulness. There are at least three benefits of crying out.

1. We tell the truth.

Sometimes when we're hurting, we are tempted to live in denial. Rejecting the reality of our pain can be a short-term coping mechanism to survive. If we try to bury our heads in the sand for very long, however, we find that we have buried our souls, and digging out feels impossible. But if we cry out to God, we tell the truth about the state of our souls and open the door to God's guidance. Proverbs 11:3 says, "Honesty guides good people; dishonesty destroys treacherous people."

2. We recognize our limits.

Pain, difficulty, and challenges remind us that we aren't invincible and that we can't handle every problem on our own. In addition to caring for ourselves and our families, many of us feel a responsibility to take care of others in our circle of influence. While that desire can be a wonderful thing, we also need to remember that we must live within the boundaries of our time, energy, resources, health, experience, and aptitude.

3. We discover we're not alone.

Crying out to God allows us to remember that at all times and in every situation, he is present with us—providing strength, wisdom, comfort, and peace. Expressing our grief also creates opportunities for compassionate friends to help shoulder our heavier burdens. When hurting, it's always tempting to believe we're suffering alone. When we express our vulnerabilities and tell our stories to trustworthy listeners, we enter into a shared experience.

The Emotions of Suffering

One of Job's gifts to us is that he teaches us how to sit with our painful emotions in the wilderness of an ash heap. How aware and connected are you to your emotional state? Many of us learn to ignore our emotions so that we can maintain some sense of control. When the realities of life feel beyond our power to rule, our emotional response is a dial that remains under our authority. Sometimes we disconnect from our emotions in order to survive difficult physical or emotional situations, to cope with loss, to avoid discomfort, or to feel powerful. In her book *Learning to Walk in the Dark*, Barbara Brown Taylor makes this observation about our emotions:

> After years of being taught that the way to deal with painful emotions is to get rid of them, it can take a lot of reschooling to learn to sit with them instead, finding out from those who feel them what they have learned by sleeping in the wilderness.[1]

Our emotions are part of who we are. Just like our bodies and minds have a need for expression, so do our emotions. The following list of eight primary emotions reveal themselves in a variety of ways to make up our "emotional range." [2]

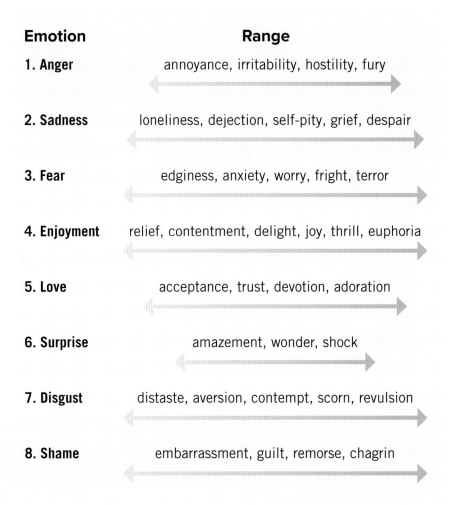

Emotion	Range
1. Anger	annoyance, irritability, hostility, fury
2. Sadness	loneliness, dejection, self-pity, grief, despair
3. Fear	edginess, anxiety, worry, fright, terror
4. Enjoyment	relief, contentment, delight, joy, thrill, euphoria
5. Love	acceptance, trust, devotion, adoration
6. Surprise	amazement, wonder, shock
7. Disgust	distaste, aversion, contempt, scorn, revulsion
8. Shame	embarrassment, guilt, remorse, chagrin

Emotions aren't good or bad—they are just expressions of the way we feel. To be a complete, whole person, we need to give words and voice to these feelings. When we close ourselves off to certain emotional expressions, those feelings find a way of leaking out. For example, do you often feel exhausted without any good reason? Do you feel lost, confused, or in a fog? Do you sense an urge to cry at unusual moments? If so, it's possible that powerful emotions are operating beneath the surface.

Expressing our emotional state helps us name our reality and invite God and others into that reality with us. Job presents a master class on expressing emotion. When his friends unanimously blame him for the evil that fell upon him , Job does not say, "Oh, I'm doing better than I deserve" or "I'm impoverished and covered in a skin disease—and everyone I love is gone—but I'm blessed!" Instead, Job erupts in volcanoes of emotion. His raw outpouring can cause us to feel uncomfortable, but it's also instructive about how to communicate with God and others.

In Peter Scazzero's book *Emotionally Healthy Spirituality*, he connects the ability to express emotions with the ability to love and to move toward spiritual health:

> To feel is to be human.... To the degree that we are unable to express our emotions, we remain impaired in our ability to love God, others, and ourselves well. Why? Because our feelings are a component of what it means to be made in the image of God. To cut them out of our spirituality is to slice off an essential part of our humanity.[3]

Job's ability to own and express his emotions creates an opportunity to grow and change. It might have been easier to fall into a trap of blame and shame, but Job demonstrates deep faith in God by faithfully confronting his painful reality.

God whispers to us in our pleasures, speaks in our conscience, but shouts in our pains: it is His megaphone to rouse a deaf world.

C. S. LEWIS, *The Problem of Pain*

Life Application Questions

1. Imagine that tragedy came to you in a similar way that it came to Job:

- Your savings, investments, or business was wiped out.

- Your children died in a tragic accident.

- Your health fell apart.

- Your spouse or most trusted friend became despondent and encouraged you to give up.

How do you think your response would compare with Job's?

2. List a couple of circumstances in your life that caused you to experience pain and suffering. How has your perspective on life and faith changed through those experiences?

3. Do you trust and love God because of the good gifts he bestows on you and others, or because of who he is and the relationship you enjoy with him? Here is a checklist to help you answer this question:

- ❏ Do I respond to difficulty by questioning God's existence, love, or goodness?

- ❏ Do I actively pursue faith in God during good *and* bad times?

- ❏ Do I process my difficult experiences *with* God, or does difficulty drive me *away* from God or his people?

- ❏ Can I look back and see how difficult experiences have deepened my faith and shaped my character?

- ❏ Am I a person who sympathizes with others in their suffering without trying to "fix" all their problems?

4. Why is presenting our pain, complaints, and honest feelings to God a faithful act of worship?

5. What difficult experiences or emotions might you still need to process with God through crying out to him?

6. Is there anyone you know who is going through a painful experience? How could you reach out and be a friend to that person and, as the apostle Paul said, "weep with those who weep" (Romans 12:15)?

Notes

2
JOB'S FRIENDS

Do We Reap
What We Sow?

Job's Friends

When Job's friends Eliphaz, Bildad, and Zophar hear what happened to Job, they come to grieve with him. For seven days and nights, they sit with Job in silence (Job 2:13). It is remarkable that Job had such supportive friends who, with no prospect of benefit, showed up in a desperate hour and silently offered support for a week.

After we read their accusations and reasoning for Job's suffering, however, we may think it would have been better if they had remained silent. They bombard Job with lengthy speeches, assuming that because their friend is suffering, he must have sinned. The story of Job challenges us to reexamine such assumptions and rethink the notion that a person always "reaps what he sows."

Read It

Key Bible Passage

Read Eliphaz's first speech and charge against Job in Job 4:1–5:27.

Optional Reading

Read Psalm 73, where the psalmist grapples with how wicked people seem to prosper.

Book of Job Reading Plan

- ❏ **Day 1:** Job chapter 8
- ❏ **Day 2:** Job chapter 9
- ❏ **Day 3:** Job chapter 10
- ❏ **Day 4:** Job chapter 11
- ❏ **Day 5:** Job chapter 12
- ❏ **Day 6:** Job chapter 13
- ❏ **Day 7:** Job chapter 14

Eliphaz the Temanite replied to Job: "When have the upright been destroyed? My experience shows that those who plant trouble and cultivate evil will harvest the same."

JOB 4:1, 7–8

Know It

1. According to Eliphaz in Job 4:7–9, what type of people experience evil, pain, and suffering? How does he describe their suffering?

2. In Job 4:18–21, what does Eliphaz believe about how God relates to the people he created?

3. *Optional Reading:* What is the psalmist's primary complaint in Psalm 73, and how does his perspective change?

The Structure of the Book of Job

Job can be divided into three sections based on literary features:

LITERARY FEATURE	DESCRIPTION	REFERENCE
1. Prose	Job's loss and the opening scene in heaven that is hidden from Job	Job 1:1–2:13
2. Poetry	The dialogues between Job and his friends and God's response to Job and his friends	Job 3:1–42:6
3. Prose	The restoration of Job's good fortune, which concludes the book	Job 42:7–17

The poetic dialogues comprise a large portion of the book, and they are mostly between Job and his three friends:

- Eliphaz the Temanite (possibly from Teman in Edom; see map in session 1)

- Bildad the Shuhite

- Zophar the Naamathite

Then enters a fourth friend who gives a long monologue in chapters 32 through 37:

- Elihu the Buzite, who is younger than the others

Finally, God's answer to Job provides a powerful conclusion to the book in chapters 38 through part of 42.

The Book of Job as Poetry and Wisdom

Job is part of the "Poetry and Wisdom" section of the Old Testament, which also includes Psalms, Proverbs, Ecclesiastes, and Song of Solomon.

- Psalms provides us with songs about life with God.

- Proverbs teaches us about the rewards of choosing wisdom.

- Ecclesiastes helps us find purpose when life feels empty.

- Song of Solomon is an intimate portrait of marriage that connects to God's relationship with his people.

These poetry and wisdom books deal with universal questions and experiences of life: joy and suffering, life and death, justice and injustice, how to gain knowledge for living well, and the many ways we can express our deepest emotions. In Proverbs and Psalms, we often find teachings about retribution. Proverbs also urges readers to choose wisdom over foolishness, because wickedness will result in suffering and misfortune:

- "The Lord curses the house of the wicked, but he blesses the home of the upright." (Proverbs 3:33)

- "The fears of the wicked will be fulfilled; the hopes of the godly will be granted." (Proverbs 10:24)

- "The one who sows iniquity will reap trouble." (Proverbs 22:8 NET)

In the book of Job, however, Job's friends take this teaching and turn it on its head. They incorrectly argue that if a person is suffering, he must have done something sinful to deserve it. The book of Job exposes the reality that there are always limits and exceptions to the principle of sowing and reaping.

Live It

Do the Wicked Prosper and the Righteous Suffer?

The shared perspective of Job's friends reveals something that many people believe without even really thinking about it: good people receive a good life from God, and bad people receive a bad life from God. Job's story challenges this assumption.

While arguing with his friends throughout the book, Job maintains his innocence and implies, at times, that either God is unjust or that he is overseeing the world and making decisions according to some principle other than justice. To successfully navigate a life of faith, we must contend with both of these faulty arguments.

A closer examination of life and the Scriptures, such as Psalm 73, reveals that many of the best people live through terrible circumstances, while people of poor character sometimes seem happy, healthy, and prosperous. Making sense of this reality is never easy, but we can see from the example of Job that often there are realities outside our perspective that influence suffering.

Perhaps the best example is Jesus Christ. Though sinless and God incarnate, for our sake he willingly suffered injustice: He died on a cross as punishment for the sins of the world. The apostle Peter explains how we are to imitate him:

> *To this you have been called, because Christ also suffered for you, leaving you an example, so that you might follow in his steps. He committed no sin, neither was deceit found in his mouth. When he was reviled, he did not revile in return; when he suffered, he did not threaten, but continued entrusting himself to him who judges justly. He himself bore our sins in his body on the tree, that we might die to sin and live to righteousness.*
>
> 1 PETER 2:21–24 ESV

Consider also these other Scriptures about suffering:

- "God blesses those who are persecuted for doing right, for the Kingdom of Heaven is theirs." (Matthew 5:10)

- "Jesus was informed that Pilate had murdered some people from Galilee as they were offering sacrifices at the Temple. 'Do you think those Galileans were worse sinners than all the other people from Galilee?' Jesus asked. 'Is that why they suffered? Not at all!'" (Luke 13:1–3)

- "Does it mean [Christ] no longer loves us if we have trouble or calamity, or are persecuted, or hungry, or destitute, or in danger, or threatened with death? ... No, despite all these things, overwhelming victory is ours through Christ, who loved us." (Romans 8:35–37)

- "It is better to suffer for doing good, if that is what God wants, than to suffer for doing wrong!" (1 Peter 3:17)

In a civilization that glorifies success and happiness and is blind to the sufferings of others, people's eyes can be opened to the truth if they remember that at the centre of the Christian faith stands an unsuccessful, tormented Christ, dying in forsakenness.

JÜRGEN MOLTMANN, *The Crucified God*

Life Application Questions

1. List a few instances where people endured suffering through no fault of their own. Next, list instances where people enjoyed good life experiences through no merit of their own.

2. How have you balanced the principle that a person "reaps what he sows" (Galatians 6:7 NIV) with the reality that sometimes people experience suffering when they have done nothing wrong?

3. List one or more Scriptures that bring you new insight or encouragement about the reality of suffering.

4. We all need the presence and support of others when we are hurting, so why do we sometimes isolate ourselves during challenging times?

5. How might you express gratitude for people who have been present for you in times of trouble?

6. Finding the right words to say to someone who is suffering can be difficult. If it were you, what kinds of statements would be helpful to hear? What would make you feel worse?

Notes

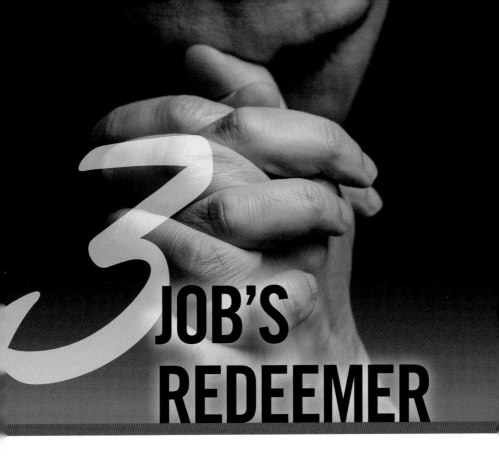

3

JOB'S REDEEMER

Keeping Faith While Suffering

Job's Redeemer

The Old Testament prophet Ezekiel mentions Job, Noah, and Daniel twice in the same chapter (Ezekiel 14:14, 20). In both instances, these three men are presented as examples of righteousness, though each lived during very challenging times:

- Noah was faithful to God while facing the scorn of others as he followed God's instructions to build an ark.

- Daniel was faithful to God while living in foreign captivity, surrounded by pressures to conform to an idolatrous religion and a corrupt political culture.

- Job remained faithful to God while experiencing the terrible loss of everything he valued.

Although words such as *faith* or *trust* are used infrequently in the book of Job, the notion of confidence in and reliance upon God runs beneath all of Job's speeches—even as he is feeling angry, hurt, and confused. It is Job's faith in God that causes him to cry out and express his innermost thoughts to God, and that same faith empowers Job to endure his suffering. Job—just like Noah and Daniel—was faithful *to* God because of his faith *in* God.

Read It

Key Bible Passage

Read Job 19:1–29 to sample more of Job's lament, followed by his unshakable statement of faith.

Optional Reading

Read a description of our future heavenly bodies from 1 Corinthians 15:35–58.

Book of Job Reading Plan

- ❑ **Day 1:** Job chapter 15
- ❑ **Day 2:** Job chapter 16
- ❑ **Day 3:** Job chapter 17
- ❑ **Day 4:** Job chapter 18
- ❑ **Day 5:** Job chapter 19
- ❑ **Day 6:** Job chapter 20
- ❑ **Day 7:** Job chapter 21

I know that my Redeemer lives, and he will stand upon the earth at last. And after my body has decayed, yet in my body I will see God!

JOB 19:25–26

1. Based on what Job says in chapter 19, what different emotions is Job feeling? List as many as you can find.

2. How does Job describe his relationship with God in verses 22 and 25–27?

3. *Optional Reading:* How does Paul's explanation of resurrected bodies, or "heavenly" bodies (1 Corinthians 15:35–58), shed light on Job's statement of faith in Job 19:25–27?

Explore It

Resurrection

After recounting more details of his terrible suffering, Job makes a remarkable statement of faith in chapter 19 that has inspired countless followers of God since: "I know that my Redeemer lives.... After my body has decayed, yet in my body I will see God!" (Job 19:25–26). Job's words compel us to hold on to hope for a glorious eternal life, no matter our circumstances. Confidence in life after death and in a coming resurrection had its origins in the Old Testament Scriptures, including Job's bold statement of faith. Here are a few other Old Testament examples of faith in resurrection:

EXAMPLE	PASSAGE
David's confidence in his future resurrection (In Acts 2:22–27, the apostle Peter said that David's statement was referring to Jesus.)	"You will not leave my soul among the dead or allow your holy one to rot in the grave. You will show me the way of life, granting me the joy of your presence and the pleasures of living with you forever." (Psalm 16:10–11)
Isaiah's confident message to the Jewish people who were facing judgment and exile	"Those who die in the Lord will live; their bodies will rise again! Those who sleep in the earth will rise up and sing for joy! For your life-giving light will fall like dew on your people in the place of the dead!" (Isaiah 26:19)
Daniel's prophecy about the end of days, the final judgment, and the general resurrection of all people—to eternal life or eternal condemnation	"At that time every one of your people whose name is written in the book will be rescued. Many of those whose bodies lie dead and buried will rise up, some to everlasting life and some to shame and everlasting disgrace." (Daniel 12:1–2)

The entire Christian faith rests on the resurrection of Jesus Christ from the dead, and the resurrection of Jesus gives us hope for our own resurrection after death—and eternal life. By the time of Jesus in the first century AD, two large schools of Jewish thought disagreed over belief in a literal, bodily resurrection. The Sadducees, who represented the ruling class of priests in Jerusalem, did not believe in a bodily resurrection. The Pharisees, who held more influence with common people as popular rabbis, scholars, and teachers, held strongly to a belief in the resurrection.

The apostle Paul had been trained as a Pharisee. After he was victimized by false accusations and stood before the Jewish ruling council, he took the opportunity to emphasize his own faith in the physical resurrection of the dead:

> *Paul realized that some members of the high council were Sadducees and some were Pharisees, so he shouted, "Brothers, I am a Pharisee, as were my ancestors! And I am on trial because my hope is in the resurrection of the dead!"*

> ACTS 23:6

Jesus not only predicted his own death and resurrection repeatedly (Matthew 16:21; 17:22–23; 20:18–19) but also raised others from the dead (Matthew 9:24–25; Luke 7:14–15; John 11:43–44). He clearly taught that the dead will be resurrected, with eternal life belonging to those who trust in him:

> *I tell you the truth, those who listen to my message and believe in God who sent me have eternal life. They will never be condemned for their sins, but they have already passed from death into life.*

> *… Don't be so surprised! Indeed, the time is coming when all the dead in their graves will hear the voice of God's Son, and they will rise again. Those who have done good will rise to experience eternal life, and those who have continued in evil will rise to experience judgment.*

> JOHN 5:24–29

Jesus told [Martha], "Your brother will rise again."

"Yes," Martha said, "he will rise when everyone else rises, at the last day."

Jesus told her, "I am the resurrection and the life. Anyone who believes in me will live, even after dying. Everyone who lives in me and believes in me will never ever die."

JOHN 11:23–26

Jesus's death and resurrection was the major theme of the apostles' teaching and of the New Testament Scriptures. Without the resurrection of Jesus, the Christian faith crumbles and becomes meaningless. Because Jesus rose from the dead, we have confidence that he will raise us from the dead too. Although Job could not have imagined the coming of Jesus and his death and resurrection, Job had hope and faith for his physical resurrection that would allow him to see God: "After my body has decayed, yet in my body I will see God! I will see him for myself. Yes, I will see him with my own eyes." Like Job, we are "overwhelmed at the thought!" (Job 19:26–27).

Live It

In the following passages, notice the way Job clarifies how (1) his trust was never in his wealth, and (2) his trust in God has not been lost along with his wealth and health:

1. "Have I put my trust in money or felt secure because of my gold?" (Job 31:24)

2. "God might kill me, but I have no other hope [but him]." (Job 13:15)

Like Job, our faith *in* God produces faithfulness *to* God in our lives. While Job was able to know and trust God, we are able to

know and trust him even more clearly than Job did. How? Through our relationship with Jesus, which expands our knowledge of God's character as well as our faith.

In times of trouble, we can cling to our faith in Jesus's righteous, loving character; his identity as God's Son; the truth of his resurrection; and his promise to resurrect his followers to eternal life. Trusting Jesus can be like an anchor that holds us steady, or a light that shines through the darkness. Here are a few principles from the New Testament that demonstrate these truths:

PRINCIPLE	NEW TESTAMENT PASSAGE
Whom we put our faith in is more important than the size of our faith.	"If you had faith even as small as a mustard seed, you could say to this mountain, 'Move from here to there,' and it would move. Nothing would be impossible." (Matthew 17:20) "If we are unfaithful, he remains faithful, for he cannot deny who he is." (2 Timothy 2:13)
Our faith is in the person of Jesus and his completed work of atonement through his death and resurrection.	"Jesus told [Martha], 'I am the resurrection and the life. Anyone who believes in me will live, even after dying. Everyone who lives in me and believes in me will never ever die.'" (John 11:25–26)
Salvation is a gift we receive by trusting Jesus.	"God saved you by his grace when you believed. And you can't take credit for this; it is a gift from God. Salvation is not a reward for the good things we have done, so none of us can boast about it." (Ephesians 2:8–9)
Faith in God's promises creates opportunity for our growth.	"Make every effort to respond to God's promises. Supplement your faith with a generous provision of moral excellence, and moral excellence with knowledge, and knowledge with self-control, and self-control with patient endurance, and patient endurance with godliness, and godliness with brotherly affection, and brotherly affection with love for everyone." (2 Peter 1:5–7)
Faith in God allows us to endure trouble and suffering.	"When troubles of any kind come your way, consider it an opportunity for great joy. For you know that when your faith is tested, your endurance has a chance to grow. So let it grow, for when your endurance is fully developed, you will be perfect and complete, needing nothing." (James 1:2–4)

I Know That My Redeemer Lives

In 1775, English pastor Samuel Medley wrote a stirring celebratory hymn based on Job's strong statement of faith in Job 19:25: "I know that my Redeemer lives."

Samuel Medley

I know that my Redeemer lives:
What joy the blest assurance gives!
He lives, He lives, who once was dead;
He lives, my everlasting Head!

He lives to bless me with His love;
He lives to plead for me above;
He lives my hungry soul to feed;
He lives to help in time of need.

He lives and grants me daily breath;
He lives and I shall conquer death;
He lives, my mansion to prepare;
He lives to bring me safely there.

He lives, all glory to His name;
He lives, my Savior, still the same;
What joy the blest assurance gives:
I know that my Redeemer lives!

[The Lord] did not say, "You shall not be tormented, you shall not be troubled, you shall not be grieved," but he said, "You shall not be overcome."

JULIAN OF NORWICH, *Revelations of Divine Love*

Life Application Questions

1. In your life experience, what has been the most difficult aspect of keeping faith while suffering?

2. If you were suffering the same things as Job (loss, grief, disease, rejection), why would believing in a future resurrection be important to you?

3. Job insists that after his death, he will see God with his own eyes (Job 19:25–27). What does this communicate about how we will experience life and our relationship with God after the resurrection?

4. What do you anticipate with the greatest joy and expectation about resurrection life with your Redeemer?

5. How does hope in a future resurrection affect your choice to submit to Jesus and the Scriptures during this life? Consider how your belief influences the following areas:

- Your values and morality:

- Your investments and generosity:

- Your suffering and difficulties:

6. What is a difficult or painful circumstance you are facing in your life now? Write a prayer to God that focuses on the following points.

- Acknowledge God's sovereign position and his goodness:

- Present your complaint or problem to him:

- Ask him to intervene:

- Express your continuing trust in him:

4
JOB'S
REFINEMENT

Enduring Trials
Patiently

Job's Refinement

The character of Job is mentioned one time in the New Testament. James, the half-brother of Jesus and leader of the early church in Jerusalem, wrote a letter to Christians who were scattered and suffering because of their faith. James encouraged these early believers to be patient, avoid complaining about each other, and confidently anticipate the Lord's kindness and eventual return. He referred to Job as an example of patient endurance:

> *For examples of patience in suffering, dear brothers and sisters, look at the prophets who spoke in the name of the Lord. We give great honor to those who endure under suffering. For instance, you know about Job, a man of great endurance.*

JAMES 5:10–11

In this session, we'll see how Job was aware that his life was thrown into the fire of testing—and how his confident, patient endurance allowed him to believe that his trial would demonstrate the strength of his character and faith.

Read It

Key Bible Passage

Read Job 23:1–17 for insights into Job's perspective and feelings during his severe trial. (As you read chapter 23, keep in mind that this is Job's answer to Eliphaz's harsh accusations in chapter 22.)

Optional Reading

Read more about life's trials and tests in James 1:2–18.

Book of Job Reading Plan

- ❏ **Day 1:** Job chapters 22–23
- ❏ **Day 2:** Job chapter 24
- ❏ **Day 3:** Job chapter 25
- ❏ **Day 4:** Job chapter 26
- ❏ **Day 5:** Job chapter 27
- ❏ **Day 6:** Job chapter 28
- ❏ **Day 7:** Job chapter 29

He [God] knows where I am going. And when he tests me, I will come out as pure as gold.

JOB 23:10

Know It

1. In Job 23:1–5, how does Job describe the way he would present his complaint to God?

2. How does Job describe his faith in God in verses 6–14?

3. How would you characterize Job's emotional state throughout this chapter?

Mining for Gold and Wisdom

When Job imagined the result of his testing, he compared his integrity and character to gold. That's a remarkable reputation—and a lofty goal for each of us!

> *[God] knows where I am going. And when he tests me, I will come out as pure as gold. For I have stayed on God's paths; I have followed his ways and not turned aside.*

> JOB 23:10–11

Gold was the most precious and rarest of materials in Job's world. In chapter 28, Job expands on this theme by comparing mining for precious stones and metals with searching for wisdom. He argues that although mining is a difficult endeavor, it is far easier than unearthing or discovering wisdom:

> *People know where to mine silver and how to refine gold. They know where to dig iron from the earth and how to smelt copper from rock.... People know how to tear apart flinty rocks and overturn the roots of mountains. They cut tunnels in the rocks and uncover precious stones.... But do people know where to find wisdom? Where can they find understanding?... It cannot be bought with gold. It cannot be purchased with silver. It's worth more than all the gold of Ophir, greater than precious onyx or lapis lazuli.*

> JOB 28:1–16

This same chapter mentions crystal, coral, jasper, and peridot. Job's speech shows that he was familiar with valuable substances and gems and the early mining practices of his day. Let's take a closer look at some of the materials he mentions:

- **Gold:** Gold was originally removed in small amounts in streams before deep mines were developed to remove it from granite veins. At times, gold and silver were found together in a mixture called electrum.

- **Iron:** Adam and Eve's son Cain had a descendant named Tubal-cain who was an early innovator in "forging tools of bronze and iron" (Genesis 4:22). Early iron use was fairly rare, because to be manipulated, iron must be heated to much higher temperatures than other metals; but after 1000 BC, iron was preferred for weapons and tools.

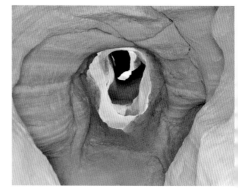
Ancient Middle Eastern copper mine

- **Copper:** Arabia and the Sinai peninsula, likely near the area where Job lived, were also home to early mining settlements, especially copper mines. Copper and tin can be combined to make bronze—a much stronger metal—but tin had to be imported from the areas now known as Afghanistan and Europe.

- **Flint:** Flint and obsidian were probably the first materials used for making tools, because they are easily found on the surface of the earth.

Paying attention to details like these can help us better understand Job's world and his knowledge of the finer and more expensive things in life, which he uses to help illustrate his testing.

Refiner's Fire

It is in our moments of severe testing—or immediately following them—that we are most likely to face our most severe temptations toward evil, with the power to wreck our lives. James explored this theme at the beginning of his letter to suffering Christians:

> Dear brothers and sisters, when **troubles** of any kind come your way, consider it an opportunity for great joy. For you know that when your faith is tested, your endurance has a chance to grow.
>
> And remember, when you are being **tempted**, do not say, "God is tempting me." God is never tempted to do wrong, and he never tempts anyone else. Temptation comes from our own desires, which entice us and drag us away.
>
> JAMES 1:2–3, 13–14

The words *troubles* and *tempted* are translations of different forms of the same Greek word: *peirasmos*. Depending on the context, this word can mean a trial or test, or it can indicate a temptation toward evil and sin.

Peirasmos is also used in ancient Greek literature to describe the refinement of gold and precious metals. When gold is mined and brought up from the earth, it's not in a pure form. To remove the other rocks and minerals, the mixture is heated up and melted down so that elements separate. The gold bubbles to the surface and is purified, or refined, as it undergoes *peirasmos*.

In the same way, God sometimes allows difficult situations in our lives for the purpose of removing evil from us, proving our faith, or testing our endurance. As Proverbs 17:3 states, "Fire tests the purity of silver and gold, but the LORD tests the heart."

Yet God never tempts us with evil. His tests are not designed to drive us toward wrongdoing or harm, but our seasons of testing can easily become twisted into temptation by the evil one. That's why 1 Peter 5:7–9 encourages us with these words:

Give all your worries and cares to God, for he cares about you. Stay alert! Watch out for your great enemy, the devil. He prowls around like a roaring lion, looking for someone to devour. Stand firm against him, and be strong in your faith. Remember that your family of believers all over the world is going through the same kind of suffering you are.

Just like a wise parent learns not to solve every problem for their child, God doesn't rescue us from every challenge. He allows us to feel resistance and hardship in order to help us grow stronger and refine our character.

Live It

The Patient Endurance of Job

Near the end of his short letter, James circles back to encouraging believers to endure hardship with patience:

- "For examples of **patience** in suffering, dear brothers and sisters, look at the prophets who spoke in the name of the Lord" (James 5:10). The word patience in this verse is a form of the Greek word *makrothumia*.

- "We give great honor to those who **endure** under suffering. For instance, you know about Job, a man of great **endurance**" (James 5:11). Endurance, another term that is connected directly to the person of Job in this passage, is a form of the Greek word *hupomoné*.

MAKROTHUMIA ("PATIENCE")	HUPOMONÉ ("ENDURANCE")
This word means forbearance, long-suffering, or the characteristic of delaying or holding back anger. It is connected with God's character and describes how he delays judgment: "The Lord isn't really being slow about his promise, as some people think. No, he is being **patient** for your sake. He does not want anyone to be destroyed, but wants everyone to repent." (2 Peter 3:9)	This word indicates a defiant perseverance against all odds and a courageous steadfastness in the face of misfortune: "You will be betrayed even by parents, brothers and sisters, other relatives, and friends.... Yet not a hair of your head will perish. By your **endurance** you will gain your lives." (Luke 21:16–19 NASB)

MAKROTHUMIA ("PATIENCE")	HUPOMONÉ ("ENDURANCE")
This word describes Jesus's patience toward sinners: "God had mercy on me so that Christ Jesus could use me as a prime example of his great **patience** with even the worst sinners." (1 Timothy 1:16)	Perseverance is possible because of the hope we have in Jesus: "In hope we were saved. Now hope that is seen is not hope, because who hopes for what he sees? But if we hope for what we do not see, we eagerly wait for it with **endurance**." (Romans 8:24–25 NET)
In the New Testament letters, this word is frequently used in lists of virtues: "The Holy Spirit produces this kind of fruit in our lives: love, joy, peace, **patience**, kindness, goodness, faithfulness, gentleness, and self-control." (Galatians 5:22–23)	This quality of patient endurance is singled out for praise by the apostle Paul: "We proudly tell God's other churches about your **endurance** and faithfulness in all the persecutions and hardships you are suffering." (2 Thessalonians 1:4)

These words illustrate the correct perspective we hope to adopt as we journey through difficult life experiences. Patiently enduring while suffering is a quality that the Holy Spirit develops in us, and it is one way that we imitate not only Job but also, and most importantly, the Lord Jesus Christ.

The Patient Endurance of Jesus

While Job demonstrated great patience and endurance, no one has ever suffered and endured in the same way that Jesus did. When he died on the cross, Jesus took on the sins of humanity and the punishment we deserved for breaking God's laws (Isaiah 53:5; Romans 3:21–26; 1 John 2:2). Jesus's suffering was infinite, because as God, he is an infinite being.

Job is a scriptural example, or "type," that foreshadows Jesus suffering innocently. Our patient endurance amid troubles, trials, and temptations can be a testimony to others of Jesus's patient endurance—and the strength he gives his followers to do the same.

Whenever we suffer, we are able to identify with Jesus. Likewise, Jesus chose to identify with us by experiencing the trials and temptations common to humanity: "[Jesus] understands our weaknesses, for he faced all of the same testings we do, yet he did not sin" (Hebrews 4:15). His example of patient endurance can strengthen us in our moments or seasons of pain.

PARALLELS BETWEEN JOB AND JESUS

Job		Jesus
"[Job] was blameless— a man of complete integrity." (Job 1:1)		"[Jesus] never sinned, nor ever deceived anyone." (1 Peter 2:22)
		"[Jesus] faced all of the same testings we do, yet he did not sin." (Hebrews 4:15)
"I have never sinned by cursing anyone or by asking for revenge." (Job 31:30)		"[Jesus] did not retaliate when he was insulted, nor threaten revenge when he suffered." (1 Peter 2:23)
"If only I knew where to find God, I would go to his court. I would lay out my case…. He would give me a fair hearing." (Job 23:3–6)		"He left his case in the hands of God, who always judges fairly." (1 Peter 2:23)

All shall work together for good: every thing is needful that he sends; nothing can be needful that he withholds.

JOHN NEWTON, *The Works of John Newton*

Life Application Questions

1. In what ways have times of hardship brought refinements and improvements to your character?

2. Describe a season of testing or trial that brought temptation with it. How did you sense God helping you overcome the enticement to sin? If you were not able to withstand the temptation, have you accepted Jesus's offer of forgiveness?

3. If Satan were to attempt to destroy your character and ruin your life, how do you imagine he might tempt you?

4. In each of the following passages, how can the principles for overcoming temptation and enduring trials help you avoid Satan's schemes?

- James 4:6–10

- 1 Peter 5:5–10

- Matthew 4:1–11

- Ephesians 6:10–18

- 1 Corinthians 10:12–13

5. When you remember that Jesus also experienced suffering, how does your view of trouble and pain change? (Consider consulting 1 Peter 4:12–19.)

6. How might you view a past, present, or current season of testing as "an opportunity for great joy" (James 1:2)?

Notes

JOB'S REALITY

The Cause and Purpose
of Suffering

Job's Reality

Near the end of the book of Job, we meet a young man named Elihu who joins the discussion between Job and his three friends. He agrees in principle with the perspective of Job's three friends—that good people receive rewards from God, while bad people receive judgment from God.

Elihu, however, takes a broader perspective by arguing that because no one is good, everyone deserves suffering. He identifies pain as a tool that can prevent people from doing bad things and claims that sometimes God teaches us wisdom through difficult experiences.

As we'll see later, in the conclusion of the book, God rebukes Job's three friends for speaking about him inaccurately, but God doesn't include Elihu in that correction. It seems that Elihu had spoken with a great deal of wisdom. Still, as you read Elihu's speech, notice how he, like Job's other friends, also fails to fully grasp Job's reality. He does not acknowledge that Job is suffering apart from any wrongdoing, and he continues to charge Job with some unknown sin.

Read It

Key Bible Passage

Read about Elihu in Job 32:1–5 and sample his speech in Job 36:1–33.

Optional Reading

Read Psalm 139, which explores God's intimate creative role in forming us and sustaining our relationship with him.

Book of Job Reading Plan

- ❏ **Day 1:** Job chapter 30
- ❏ **Day 2:** Job chapter 31
- ❏ **Day 3:** Job chapter 32
- ❏ **Day 4:** Job chapter 33
- ❏ **Day 5:** Job chapter 34
- ❏ **Day 6:** Job chapter 35
- ❏ **Day 7:** Job chapters 36–37

Look, God is all-powerful. Who is a teacher like him? No one can tell him what to do, or say to him, "You have done wrong." Instead, glorify his mighty works, singing songs of praise.

JOB 36:22–24

Know It

1. Why is Elihu so angry, and what is he trying to accomplish with his speech to Job?

2. How would you describe Elihu's perspective on God's relationship with people and with creation?

3. *Optional Reading:* In Psalm 139:1–12, what do you observe about God's presence and participation in our lives?

Views on Suffering

Various worldviews, cultures, and faiths present their own unique views on suffering and pain. While we can respect different traditions, it's important to hold strongly to thoroughly biblical beliefs. Comparing and contrasting the Christian view with other perspectives can help us more clearly understand and live out our faith in Jesus when we have painful experiences:

Non-Christian Views on Suffering[4]

BUDDHISM	ISLAM
Suffering isn't real but grows from our state of mind as we are inappropriately attached to people, things, and desires. *(Not Real)*	Suffering is the fate or destiny of some people, and it cannot be changed. *(Fatalism)*
HINDUISM	**SECULARISM**
Suffering is the result of evil that you have committed in this life or a previous life. *(Karma)*	Suffering is random, something to be avoided or overcome, and absolutely without any meaning. *(No Purpose)*

Contrary to the views above, the Bible teaches that suffering is real, often unfair, and sometimes overwhelming—but never without purpose. Pastor Tim Keller, in his book *Walking with God through Pain and Suffering*, said it so well: "Christianity teaches us that, contra fatalism, suffering is overwhelming; contra Buddhism, suffering is real; contra karma, suffering is often unfair; but contra secularism, suffering is meaningful."[5]

Christian Views on Suffering

Suffering is real.

"Here on earth you will have many trials and sorrows."
(John 16:33)

Suffering is often unfair.

"God is pleased when, conscious of his will, you patiently endure unjust treatment." (1 Peter 2:19)

Sometimes suffering is overwhelming.

"I am overwhelmed with troubles and my life draws near to death." (Psalm 88:3 NIV)

Suffering is never without purpose.

"Our present troubles are small and won't last very long. Yet they produce for us a glory that vastly outweighs them and will last forever!"
(2 Corinthians 4:17)

God is able to bring good out of our painful experiences by working them into his plans for our lives. Our troubles and challenges can grow our faith and stimulate our hope, as the apostle Paul explained in his letter to the Roman church:

We believers also groan, even though we have the Holy Spirit within us as a foretaste of future glory, for we long for our bodies to be released from sin and suffering....

... And we know that God causes everything to work together for the good of those who love God and are called according to his purpose for them. For God knew his people in advance, and he chose them to become like his Son, so that his Son would be the firstborn among many brothers and sisters. And having chosen them, he called them to come to him. And having called them, he gave them right standing with himself. And having given them right standing, he gave them his glory.

ROMANS 8:23–30

Biblical Examples of Suffering

From where does our suffering come? Why do we experience pain, and why are people who are no more wicked than anyone else plagued with difficult trials? The book of Job offers some insight into these questions, but we can find more clues in other parts of the Bible. Throughout the Scriptures, different possible causes and purposes are presented:

REASON	EXAMPLE
To correct or to discipline disobedience or harmful actions	When the prophet Jonah disobeyed God's command to preach in Nineveh, he endured a violent storm and was swallowed by a giant fish (Jonah 1–2).
As a natural result of our poor decisions	Many times, wrongdoing brings its own painful consequences. King David's son Absalom experienced this when he died in battle after rebelling against David's authority (2 Samuel 15–18).
Opposition from Satan	Job himself is the prime example in the Scriptures. Satan harassed Job and attempted to prove that his faith in God was only due to his health and wealth (Job 1–2).
The natural state of our broken world	In a world marred by sin, bad and unfair events can occur at any time to anyone (Luke 13:1–5).
To achieve a future higher purpose and good	Joseph was sold into slavery and endured unjust imprisonment, which ultimately allowed him to become an important official in Egypt and rescue multitudes from famine, including his family (Genesis 37; 39–42).

REASON	EXAMPLE
To strengthen our dependence on and love for God	The apostle Paul experienced "a thorn in [the] flesh" (an unspecified painful experience) that caused him to depend on the Lord and grow in humility as Jesus was glorified through his ministry (2 Corinthians 12:1–10).
The expansion of our witness that Jesus is the Son of God and offers salvation	Paul and Silas were arrested and imprisoned unjustly, but God used that event to help the jailer and his family hear the good news about Jesus (Acts 16:16–34).
For God's glory and our sharing with him in that glory	The apostles often encouraged persecuted believers with the hope that they were honoring God through their sufferings, as well as investing in their own future glory when Christ returns (Romans 8:17–18; 1 Peter 4:12–19).

It's clear there are many possible reasons behind our experiences with pain, so discerning the correct one can be difficult or impossible. As we'll see later, at the conclusion of Job's story, there is no indication that Job ever learned the cause of his suffering or became aware of the conversations between God and Satan. Job lived the rest of his life unaware of any reason for his terrible misfortune. Like Job, we may never receive the answers we desire during this life, and trying to pinpoint the source of our hardships can be counterproductive or even harmful.

Elihu communicated to Job significant truths about God's work in our world, God's wisdom, and God's power, but he still fell short of really understanding Job's situation. Although it is admirable to try to help others, we are wise to be very cautious when diagnosing the causes and purposes behind other people's problems. As chapters 1 and 2 of Job demonstrate, only the Lord knows all the hidden factors that influence the circumstances of our lives.

Live It

Suffering Transforms Us

The reality of life is that our stories will include some chapters of disappointment and pain. Job's certainly did. Yet at the end of his story, Job was a very different person than he was at the beginning. The same can be true for every person who goes through hardship.

Enduring through the realities and difficulties of life develops in us a deeper quality of authenticity. *The Velveteen Rabbit*, a classic story for children, illustrates this principle with a timeless message that also instructs adults. The paraphrased excerpt below contains a revealing dialogue between a new toy—a fluffy rabbit—and an old horse toy:

> Rabbit asks Horse, "What is REAL? ... Does it mean having things that buzz inside you and a stick-out handle?"
>
> "Real isn't how you are made," answers Horse. "It's a thing that happens to you. When a child loves you for a long, long time, not just to play with, but REALLY loves you, then you become Real."
>
> "Does it hurt?" asks Rabbit.
>
> "Sometimes," Horse replies, since he was always truthful. "When you are Real, you don't mind being hurt."
>
> "Does it happen all at once, like being wound up? ... Or bit by bit?" asks Rabbit.
>
> "It doesn't happen all at once," says Horse. "You become. It takes a long time. That's why it doesn't often happen to people who break easily, or have sharp edges, or who have to be carefully kept. Generally, by the time you are Real, most of your hair has been loved off and your eyes drop out and you

get loose in the joints and very shabby. But these things don't matter at all, because once you are Real you can't be ugly, except to people who don't understand."

Walking through times of pain and suffering does the work of making us real. As our sharp edges are worn away and the attractive veneer we work so hard to present to others is rubbed off by the friction of life, we are transformed into the person God calls us to be. Job's process of "becoming" has been recorded for our benefit, and we are all on a similar journey to become more like Jesus through the challenges we experience. Suffering doesn't invalidate the reality of God and his goodness; it simply means that we are truly experiencing life.

If faced rightly, [suffering] can drive us like a nail deep into the love of God and into more stability and spiritual power than you can imagine.

TIM KELLER, *Walking with God through Pain and Suffering*

Life Application Questions

1. What are some of God's purposes for our lives? How might seasons of testing accomplish those purposes?

2. In what ways have you experienced God's presence and guidance during times of pain or suffering?

3. How have life's difficulties motivated you toward growth and becoming more like Jesus?

4. Many of our difficult experiences are the result of the actions of others. What steps might you take to seek healing for yourself and extend forgiveness to someone who has wounded you?

5. When you're facing difficulties in life, what things, or which people, help you hang on to hope?

6. Have you ever thanked God for events you would consider unfortunate? Write a note or offer a prayer that expresses gratitude for the positive ways those experiences have impacted you.

Notes

GOD'S ANSWER

*Trusting in God's
Sovereignty*

God's Answer

At the end of the book of Job, God responds to Job's accusations of injustice. God never actually informs Job about why he has suffered so greatly. Instead, he asks Job a series of questions about the wonders of the natural world.

Through his questions, God teaches Job that the divine perspective is far above any arguments that Job can claim. God clarifies with Job that in no way has he acted unjustly. Rather, Job's accusation of God's injustice is itself unfair.

The overarching theme of God's communication with Job is that God is sovereign over the natural world, the forces of chaos and destruction, and even Job's life. God is the supreme King who reigns and rules over all. This truth is mysterious, confusing, and comforting.

Read It

Key Bible Passage

Read Job 38:1–21 to sample God's response to Job, and Job 42:1–17, where Job responds to God and God blesses Job.

Optional Reading

Read Psalm 29, a song about God's majesty and power.

Book of Job Reading Plan

- ❏ **Day 1:** Job chapter 38
- ❏ **Day 2:** Job chapter 39
- ❏ **Day 3:** Job chapter 40
- ❏ **Day 4:** Job chapter 41
- ❏ **Day 5:** Job chapter 42

I had only heard about you before, but now I have seen you with my own eyes. I take back everything I said, and I sit in dust and ashes to show my repentance.

JOB 42:5–6

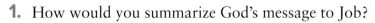

Know It

1. How would you summarize God's message to Job?

2. How is Job's perspective different in chapter 42 than in earlier parts of the book?

3. What do you think the epilogue in Job 42:10–17 communicates about Job's character and his trials?

Leviathan and Behemoth

In chapters 38–41, God takes Job on a tour of the natural world to demonstrate his authority over creation and his magnificent power and wisdom. Two examples God provides are in his relationship with creatures called "Behemoth" and "Leviathan." The modern identity of both remains shrouded in mystery.

Leviathan (Job 41), a menacing creature that can't be tamed by people, is characterized by:

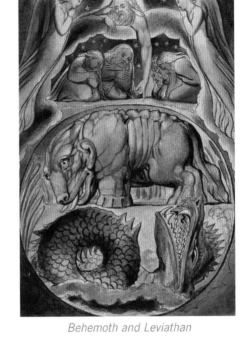

Behemoth and Leviathan

- "Terrible" teeth (v. 14)

- Impenetrable scales (vv. 15–17)

- Fiery breath (vv. 18–21)

- Easily defeats warriors (vv. 25–29)

- Able to break iron and bronze (v. 27)

- King of the beasts (v. 34)

Behemoth's description is short but also impressive (Job 40):

- Powerful loins, muscles, tail, bones, and limbs (vv. 16–18)

- Thrives in mountainous areas and near rivers (vv. 20–23)

- Threatened by no one but God himself (vv. 19, 24)

Some Bible scholars have suggested that Leviathan could have been a crocodile and Behemoth a hippopotamus or rhinoceros, but those comparisons seem to fall far short of the description in Job. Others have suggested the possibility of dinosaurs. Both Isaiah and the Psalms also mention Leviathan:

> In that day the LORD will take his terrible, swift sword and punish Leviathan, the swiftly moving serpent, the coiling, writhing serpent. He will kill the dragon of the sea.
>
> ISAIAH 27:1

> You crushed the heads of Leviathan
>   and let the desert animals eat him.
>
> PSALM 74:14, BY ASAPH

> See the ships sailing along,
>   and Leviathan, which you made to play in the sea.
>
> PSALM 104:26

The ancient cultures that surrounded the people of Israel told stories about mythological creatures their gods battled and tamed: Canaanites told stories about Baal battling and overcoming a Leviathan-like dragon, and Babylonians created myths about their gods defeating similar monsters of chaos. (Writers like Asaph in Psalms and the prophet Isaiah may have used the imagery of Leviathan to describe Israel's enemies, who, like the old mythical beasts, were committed to destruction.)

In the book of Job, however, God doesn't battle Leviathan or Behemoth or treat them like chaos monsters. This is very different from the mythology of Israel's neighbors. Instead, God's speech to Job reveals beauty and power in these formidable beasts who exist in submission to God's authority. Leviathan and Behemoth are awe-inspiring creatures who are capable of spreading terror, but they are also examples of God's unlimited power and control over the world he created.

God's Assessment of Job and His Friends

In Job chapter 42, God affirms Job for speaking accurately about him. God also addresses Job's friend Eliphaz and announces he is angry with him and Job's other two friends, Bildad and Zophar, because they spoke about him inaccurately. Think back through what has happened throughout the book. Job repeatedly complained that God treated him unfairly, so he demanded to present his case directly to God. Eventually, God spoke to Job out of a whirlwind. Although God never directly answered Job's questions and accusation, he humbled Job by the demonstration and explanation of his awesome power and unrivaled position.

Job's three friends devoted their speeches to defending God to Job and reasoning how God was correct to punish Job. God spent four chapters rebuking Job but ultimately praised Job for speaking about him correctly. This is all a bit confusing, but it seems clear that all of Job's complaints were delivered from a heart of faith. Job never stopped wanting to talk with God, wrestling with God, opening up his heart to God, and verbalizing exactly what was on his mind. Job continued trusting God and kept open lines of communication, even when he felt he was being treated unfairly. It seems that God isn't looking for defenders as much as he is looking for faith and honesty—even amid confusion and pain.

Praying for Others

Often overlooked because of the tragedy of Job's story is the spiritual leadership Job provided for his family and friends. In the first chapter of the book, we see that although Job's children were grown and living on their own, he was still invested in their spiritual lives:

> Job's sons would take turns preparing feasts in their homes, and they would also invite their three sisters to celebrate with them. When these celebrations ended—sometimes after several days—Job would purify his children. He would get up early in the morning and offer a burnt offering for each of them. For Job said to himself, "Perhaps my children have sinned and have cursed God in their hearts." This was Job's regular practice.
>
> JOB 1:4–5

Job was likely continuing a habit of prayer and sacrifice that began when his children were young. It was costly, but he was willing to give his best to benefit his children's relationship with God. Now, at the end of the book, we see Job interceding for others once again. After God rebuked Job's friends and told them to repent by bringing sacrifices, he stated that Job would pray for them:

> Take seven bulls and seven rams and go to my servant Job and offer a burnt offering for yourselves. My servant Job will pray for you, and I will accept his prayer on your behalf.
>
> JOB 42:8

In Job's intercession for others, we see additional parallels between Job and the ministry of Jesus, who intercedes on our behalf:

> Jesus died for us and was raised to life for us, and he is sitting in the place of honor at God's right hand, pleading for us.
>
> ROMANS 8:34

[Jesus] is able, once and forever, to save those who come to God through him. He lives forever to intercede with God on their behalf.

HEBREWS 7:25

If anyone does sin, we have an advocate who pleads our case before the Father. He is Jesus Christ, the one who is truly righteous.

1 JOHN 2:1

Following in Job's Footsteps

Job is a wonderful example for any parent, grandparent, aunt or uncle, or friend. We have a responsibility to pass our faith on to future generations, and it is our privilege to pray that those we care about will have a right relationship with God. This responsibility endures throughout our lifetime. Consider taking the following points of action to follow in Job's footsteps:

- If you had family members or friends who prayed for you and guided you toward faith in Christ, take time to express your gratitude to them. If they are still living, call or send a card, a letter, or an email. Even better, if possible, get together in person for coffee or a meal. If they have passed away, take some time to thank God for them.

- Pray for the young people in your life to have hearts that seek Jesus.

- Besides prayer, brainstorm a few steps you can take to shepherd their hearts toward Jesus (for example, give them a Bible; invite them to church; complete a Bible study together).

God's Sovereignty

The book of Job does not answer the question of why suffering exists. Instead, the book shows that trusting in God's sovereign wisdom, power, and goodness is a better comfort to those who suffer than having an answer. Consider these principles that inform our understanding about God's sovereignty:

- **God's wisdom is beyond our understanding.**

  "My ways are higher than your ways and my thoughts higher than your thoughts." (Isaiah 55:9)

- **God's plans will always be completed.**

  "You can do anything, and no one can stop you." (Job 42:2)

  "The LORD's plans stand firm forever; his intentions can never be shaken." (Psalm 33:11)

- **God will establish his kingdom to complete human history.**

  "God's home is now among his people! ... God himself will be with them. He will wipe every tear from their eyes." (Revelation 21:3–4)

Because God is sovereign, we can trust him even when we're hurting and confused by the events in our lives.

Pain and suffering have to come into your life, but remember: Pain, sorrow, suffering are but the kiss of Jesus—signs that you have come so close to Him that He can kiss you.

MOTHER TERESA, *Love: A Fruit Always in Season*

Life Application Questions

1. God rebukes Job's three friends but rewards Job. What do you learn about God's character from his speech to Job and his restoration of Job?

2. Why do you think that God doesn't really answer Job's question about why innocent people suffer?

3. Make two lists: the first noting the bad events of your life, and the second noting the good ones. Have any of your greatest experiences grown out of your most miserable events? How can this comparison help you trust God's sovereignty in every season of life?

BAD EVENTS	GOOD EVENTS

4. Like Job who prayed on behalf of his children and friends, list some people who need God in their lives that you can pray for.

Family	
Friends	
Church and Community	
Nation and World	

5. Where do you most recognize God's majesty and power in the natural world? What inspires awe in you?

6. What questions still exist in your mind about trouble and pain or about the story of Job? How has your view of suffering changed through studying the book of Job?

Notes

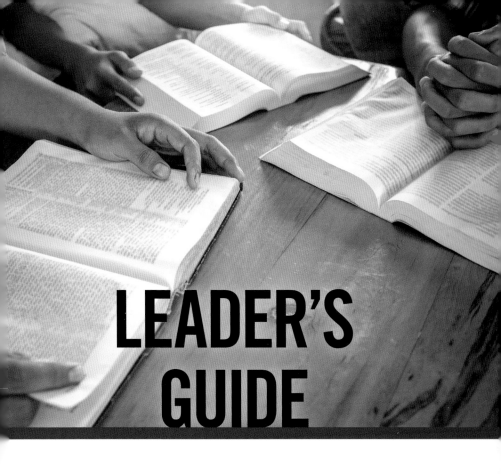

LEADER'S GUIDE

"Encourage one another and build each other up."

1 THESSALONIANS 5:11

Leader's Guide

Congratulations! You've either decided to lead a Bible study, or you're thinking hard about it. Guess what? God does big things through small groups. When his people gather together, open his Word, and invite his Spirit to work, their lives are changed!

Do you feel intimidated yet?

Be comforted by this: even the great apostle Paul felt "in over his head" at times. When he went to Corinth to help people grasp God's truth, he admitted he was overwhelmed: "I came to you in weakness with great fear and trembling" (1 Corinthians 2:3). Later he wondered, "Who is adequate for such a task as this?" (2 Corinthians 2:16 NLT).

Feelings of inadequacy are normal; every leader has them. What's more, they're actually healthy. They keep us dependent on the Lord. It is in our times of greatest weakness that God works most powerfully. The Lord assured Paul, "My grace is sufficient for you, for my power is made perfect in weakness" (2 Corinthians 12:9).

The Goal

What is the goal of a Bible study group? Listen as the apostle Paul speaks to Christians:

- "Oh, my dear children! I feel as if I'm going through labor pains for you again, and they will continue until *Christ is fully developed in your lives*" (Galatians 4:19 NLT, emphasis added).

- "For God knew his people in advance, and he chose them *to become like his Son*" (Romans 8:29 NLT, emphasis added).

Do you see it? God's ultimate goal for us is that we would become like Jesus Christ. This means a Bible study is not about filling our heads with more information. Rather, it is about undergoing transformation. We study and apply God's truth so that it will reshape our hearts and minds, and so that over time, we will become more and more like Jesus.

Paul said, "The purpose of my instruction is that all believers would be filled with love that comes from a pure heart, a clear conscience, and genuine faith" (1 Timothy 1:5 NLT).

This isn't about trying to "master the Bible." No, we're praying that God's Word will master us, and through humble submission to its authority, we'll be changed from the inside out.

Your Role

Many group leaders experience frustration because they confuse their role with God's role. Here's the truth: God alone knows our deep hang-ups and hurts. Only he can save a soul, heal a heart, fix a life. It is God who rescues people from depression, addictions, bitterness, guilt, and shame. We Bible study leaders need to realize that *we can't do any of those things.*

So what can we do? More than we think!

- We can pray.

- We can trust God to work powerfully.

- We can obey the Spirit's promptings.

- We can prepare for group gatherings.

- We can keep showing up faithfully.

With group members:

- We can invite, remind, encourage, and love.

- We can ask good questions and then listen attentively.

- We can gently speak tough truths.

- We can celebrate with those who are happy and weep with those who are sad.

- We can call and text and let them know we've got their back.

But we can never do the things that only the Almighty can do.

- We can't play the Holy Spirit in another person's life.

- We can't be in charge of outcomes.

- We can't force God to work according to our timetables.

And one more important reminder: besides God's role and our role, group members also have a key role to play in this process. If they don't show up, prepare, or open their hearts to God's transforming truth, no life change will take place. We're not called to manipulate or shame, pressure or arm twist. We're not to blame if members don't make progress—and we don't get the credit when they do. We're mere instruments in the hands of God.

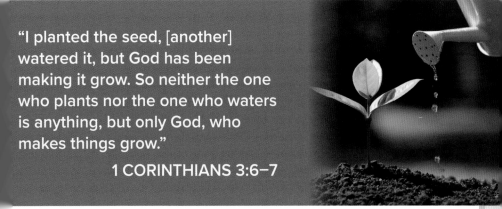

"I planted the seed, [another] watered it, but God has been making it grow. So neither the one who plants nor the one who waters is anything, but only God, who makes things grow."
1 CORINTHIANS 3:6–7

Leader Myths and Truths

Many people assume that a Bible study leader should:

- Be a Bible scholar.

- Be a dynamic communicator.

- Have a big, fancy house to meet in.

- Have it all together—no doubts, bad habits, or struggles.

These are myths—even outright lies of the enemy!

Here's the truth:

- God is looking for humble Bible students, not scholars.

- You're not signing up to give lectures, you're agreeing to facilitate discussions.

- You don't need a palace, just a place where you can have uninterrupted discussions. (Perhaps one of your group members will agree to host your study.)

- Nobody has it all together. We are all in process. We are all seeking to work out "our salvation with fear and trembling" (Philippians 2:12).

As long as your desire is that Jesus be Lord of your life, God will use you!

- You want to wow others with your biblical knowledge.

  "Love . . . does not boast, it is not proud"
  (1 Corinthians 13:4).

- You're seeking a hidden personal gain or profit.

  "We do not peddle the word of God for profit"
  (2 Corinthians 2:17).

- You want to tell people how wrong they are.

  "Do not condemn" (Romans 2:1).

- You want to fix or rescue people.

  "It is God who works in you to will and to act"
  (Philippians 2:13).

- You're being pressured to do it.

  "Am I now trying to win the approval of
  human beings, or of God?" (Galatians 1:10).

A Few Do's

✔ Pray for your group.

Are you praying for your group members regularly? It is the most important thing a leader can do for his or her group.

✔ Ask for help.

If you're new at leading, spend time with an experienced group leader and pick his or her brain.

✔ Encourage members to prepare.

Challenge participants to read the Bible passages and the material in their study guides, and to answer and reflect on the study questions during the week prior to meeting.

✔ Discuss the group guidelines.

Go over important guidelines with your group at the first session, and again as needed if new members join the group in later sessions. See the *Group Guidelines* at the end of this leader's guide.

✔ Share the load.

Don't be a one-person show. Ask for volunteers. Let group members host the meeting, arrange for snacks, plan socials, lead group prayer times, and so forth. The old saying is true: Participants become boosters; spectators become critics.

✔ Be flexible.

If a group member shows up in crisis, it is okay to stop and take time to surround the hurting brother or sister with love. Provide a safe place for sharing. Listen and pray for his or her needs.

✔ Be kind.

Remember, there's a story—often a heart-breaking one—behind every face. This doesn't *excuse* bad or disruptive behavior on the part of group members, but it might *explain* it.

A Few Don'ts

✘ Don't "wing it."

Although these sessions are designed to require minimum preparation, read each one ahead of time. Highlight the questions you feel are especially important for your group to spend time on.

✘ Don't feel ashamed to say, "I don't know."

Disciple means "learner," not "know-it-all."

✘ Don't feel the need to "dump the truck."

You don't have to say everything you know. There is always next week. A little silence during group discussion time, that's fine. Let members wrestle with questions.

✘ Don't put members on the spot.

Invite others to share and pray, but don't pressure them. Give everyone an opportunity to participate. People will open up on their own time as they learn to trust the group.

✘ Don't go down "rabbit trails."

Be careful not to let one person dominate the time or for the discussion to go down the gossip road. At the same time, don't short-circuit those occasions when the Holy Spirit is working in your group members' lives and therefore they *need* to share a lot.

✘ Don't feel pressure to cover every question.

Better to have a robust discussion of four questions than a superficial conversation of ten.

✘ Don't go long.

Encourage good discussion, but don't be afraid to "rope 'em back in" when needed. Start and end on time. If you do this from the beginning, you'll avoid the tendency of group members to arrive later and later as the season goes on.

How to Use This Study Guide

Many group members have busy lives—dealing with long work hours, childcare, and a host of other obligations. These sessions are designed to be as simple and straightforward as possible to fit into a busy schedule. Nevertheless, encourage group members to set aside some time during the week (even if it's only a little) to pray, read the key Bible passage, and respond to questions in this study guide. This will make the group discussion and experience much more rewarding for everyone.

Each session contains four parts.

Read It

The *Key Bible Passage* is the portion of Scripture everyone should read during the week before the group meeting. The group can read it together at the beginning of the session as well.

The *Optional Reading* is for those who want to dig deeper and read lengthier Bible passages on their own during the week.

Know It

This section encourages participants to reflect on the Bible passage they've just read. Here, the goal is to interact with the biblical text and grasp what it says. (We'll get into practical application later.)

Explore It

Here group members can find background information with charts and visuals to help them understand the Bible passage and the topic more deeply. They'll move beyond the text itself and see how it connects to other parts of Scripture and the historical and cultural context.

Live It

Finally, participants will examine how God's Word connects to their lives. There are application questions for group discussion or personal reflection, practical ideas to apply what they've learned from God's Word, and a closing thought and/or prayer. (Remember, you don't have to cover all the questions or everything in this section during group time. Focus on what's most important for your group.)

Celebrate!

Here's an idea: Have a plan for celebrating your time together after the last session of this Bible study. Do something special after your gathering time, or plan a separate celebration for another time and place. Maybe someone in your group has the gift of hospitality—let them use their gifting and organize the celebration.

	30-MINUTE SESSION	60-MINUTE SESSION
READ IT	Open in prayer and read the *Key Bible Passage.* 5 minutes	Open in prayer and read the *Key Bible Passage.* 5 minutes
KNOW IT	Ask: "What stood out to you from this Bible passage?" 5 minutes	Ask: "What stood out to you from this Bible passage?" 5 minutes
EXPLORE IT	Encourage group members to read this section on their own, but don't spend group time on it. Move on to the life application questions.	Ask: "What did you find new or helpful in the *Explore It* section? What do you still have questions about?" 10 minutes
LIVE IT	Members voluntarily share their answers to 3 or 4 of the life application questions. 15 minutes	Members voluntarily share their answers to the life application questions. 25 minutes
PRAYER & CLOSING	Conclude with a brief prayer. 5 minutes	Share prayer requests and praise reports. Encourage the group to pray for each other in the coming week. Conclude with a brief prayer. 15 minutes

Open in prayer and read the *Key Bible Passage.*

5 minutes

- Ask: "What stood out to you from this Bible passage?"

- Then go over the *Know It* questions as a group.

10 minutes

- Ask: "What did you find new or helpful in the *Explore It* section? What do you still have questions about?"

- Here, the leader can add information found while preparing for the session.

- If there are questions or a worksheet in this section, go over those as a group.

20 minutes

- Members voluntarily share their answers to the life application questions.

- Wrap up this time with a closing thought or suggestions for how to put into practice in the coming week what was just learned from God's Word.

30 minutes

- Share prayer requests and praise reports.

- Members voluntarily pray during group time about the requests and praises shared.

- Encourage the group to pray for each other in the coming week.

25 minutes

Group Guidelines

This group is about discovering God's truth, supporting each other, and finding growth in our new life in Christ. To reach these goals, a group needs a few simple guidelines that everyone should follow for the group to stay healthy and for trust to develop.

1. **Everyone agrees to make group time a priority.**
   We understand that there are work, health, and family issues that come up. So if there is an emergency or schedule conflict that cannot be avoided, be sure to let someone know that you can't make it that week. This may seem like a small thing, but it makes a big difference to your other group members.

2. **What is said in the group stays in the group.**
   Accept it now: we are going to share some personal things. Therefore, the group must be a safe and confidential place to share.

3. **Don't be judgmental, even if you strongly disagree.**
   Listen first, and contribute your perspective only as needed. Remember, you don't fully know someone else's story. Take this advice from James: "Be quick to listen, slow to speak, and slow to become angry" (James 1:19).

4. **Be patient with one another.**
   We are all in process, and some of us are hurting and struggling more than others. Don't expect bad habits or attitudes to disappear overnight.

5. **Everyone participates.**
   It may take time to learn how to share, but as you develop a trust toward the other group members, take the chance.

If you struggle in any of these areas, ask God's help for growth, and ask the group to help hold you accountable. Remember, you're all growing together.

Notes

1 Barbara Brown Taylor, *Learning to Walk in the Dark* (Norwich, England: Canterbury, 2014), 86.

2 Adapted from Daniel Goleman, *Emotional Intelligence* (New York: Bantam Dell, 2006), 289–90.

3 Peter Scazzero, *Emotionally Healthy Spirituality* (Grand Rapids, MI: Zondervan, 2017), 24–25.

4 Adapted from Timothy Keller, *Walking with God through Pain and Suffering* (New York: Riverhead, 2015), 30.

5 Keller, *Walking with God through Pain and Suffering*, 30.

Image Credits

Relief map on p. 14 by Michael Schmeling, http://www.aridocean.com.

Images used under license from Shutterstock.com: book, light bulb, compass, and plant icons: Happy Art; Sergey Shubin, pp. 3, 7, 22; Bits And Splits, pp. 3, 27, 34; StockPhotosArt, pp. 3, 39, 48; mehmetcan, pp. 3, 53, 64; Darkdiamond67, pp. 3, 69, 78; Paul Shuang, pp. 3, 83, 92; Chat Karen Studio, pp. 3, 97; Radek Borovka, p. 5; Oliver Denker, p. 5; Seregam, pp. 8, 26, 28, 38, 40, 52, 54, 68, 70, 82, 84; Ilan Ejzykowicz, p. 13; melhijad, p. 29; j.chizhe, p. 41; Rachata Sinthopachakul, p. 45; Suzanne Tucker, p. 46; Aleksandra Tregubovich, p. 55; Finesell, p. 57; Mali lucky, p. 57; Bjoern Wylezich, p. 57; Africa Studio, p. 57; Ground Picture, p. 63; Javier Cruz Acosta, p. 71; Denis Belitsky, p. 85; Sabphoto, p. 89; P Maxwell Photography, pp. 98, 108, 109; amenic181, p. 101; Keep Smiling Photography, p. 103.

Other images: Gonzalo Carrasco, Job on the Dunghill—Google Art Project, Wikimedia Commons, p. 9; James Jacques Joseph Tissot, Job and His Three Friends—Gifts of the heirs of Jacob Schiff, Jewish Museum, p. 18; Portrait of Samuel Medley—Wikimedia Commons, p. 48; Copper mines, Timna Valley, Negev Desert, Israel—Zairon, Wikimedia Commons, p. 58 (https://creativecommons.org/licenses/by -sa/4.0/deed.en); Behemoth and Leviathan—Yale Center for British Art, Paul Mellon Collection (public domain), p. 87.

ROSE VISUAL BIBLE STUDIES
6-Session Study Guides for Personal or Group Use

THE BOOK OF JAMES
Find out how to cultivate a living faith through six tests of faith.

THE TABERNACLE
Discover how each item of the tabernacle foreshadowed Jesus.

THE ARMOR OF GOD
Dig deep into Ephesians 6 and learn the meaning of each piece of the armor.

THE LIFE OF PAUL
See how the apostle Paul persevered through trials and proclaimed the gospel.

JOURNEY TO THE RESURRECTION
Renew your heart and mind as you engage in spiritual practices. Perfect for Easter.

I AM
Know the seven powerful claims of Christ from the gospel of John.

THE TWELVE DISCIPLES
Learn about the twelve men Jesus chose to be his disciples.

PROVERBS
Gain practical, godly wisdom from the book of Proverbs.

WOMEN OF THE BIBLE: OLD TESTAMENT
Journey through six inspiring stories of women of courage and wisdom.

WOMEN OF THE BIBLE: NEW TESTAMENT
See women's impact in the ministry of Jesus and the early church.

THE LORD'S PRAYER
Deepen your prayer life with the seven petitions in the Lord's Prayer.

FRUIT OF THE SPIRIT
Explore the nine spiritual fruits.

PSALMS
Discover the wild beauty of praise.

THE EXODUS
Witness God's mighty acts in the exodus.

THE BOOK OF JOB
Explore questions about faith and suffering.

www.hendricksonrose.com